Tombs
of the
Vanishing
Indian

MARIE CLEMENTS

Talonbooks

Talonbooks
278 East First Avenue, Vancouver, British Columbia, Canada v5t 1a6
www.talonbooks.com

Second printing: November 2017

Typeset in Minion and printed and bound in Canada.
Printed on 100% post-consumer recycled paper.
Typeset by Typesmith. Cover design by Overleaf.

Talonbooks acknowledges the financial support of the Canada Council for the Arts, the Government of Canada through the Canada Book Fund, and the Province of British Columbia through the British Columbia Arts Council and the Book Publishing Tax Credit.

Canada Conseil des arts Canada Council BRITISH BRITISH COLUMBIA
du Canada for the Arts COLUMBIA ARTS COUNCIL

LIBRARY AND ARCHIVES CANADA CATALOGUING IN PUBLICATION

Clements, Marie, 1962–

   Tombs of the vanishing Indian / Marie Clements.

A play.

ISBN 978-0-88922-686-9

   I. Title.

PS8555.L435T64 2012   C812'.6   C2011-908723-5

Tombs of the Vanishing Indian

PRODUCTION HISTORY

Tombs of the Vanishing Indian was commissioned to mark the tenth anniversary of the Native Voices series at the Autry National Center and the Southwest Museum of the American Indian in Los Angeles. Given an extended research and writer's retreat and workshop at Native Voices in 2004 and 2005, *Tombs of the Vanishing Indian* was presented as a staged reading in November 2005 at Live at the Autry in Los Angeles.

Additional staged readings were performed at La Jolla Playhouse on Saturday, June 5, and at the Autry National Center on Saturday, June 26, 2010.

DIRECTOR: Seema Sueko
DRAMATURG: Brian Quirt

Tombs of the Vanishing Indian was first performed in a Native Earth Performing Arts and red diva projects co-production at Buddies in Bad Times Theatre in Toronto from March 9 to March 27, 2011.

JESSIE: Nicole Joy-Fraser
MIRANDA: Falen Johnson
JANEY: PJ Prudat
THE MOTHER / THE LONE WOMAN / RUTH / SARAH:
    Michelle St. John
DR. DANIEL HANSEN / BLACKCOAT THREE:
    Keith Barker
BOB STILLS / BLACKCOAT TWO / WHITE INTERN ONE:
    David Storch
DETECTIVE FULLEN / BLACKCOAT ONE / WHITE INTERN TWO:
    Martin Julien

DIRECTOR: Yvette Nolan
SET DESIGN: Jackie Chau
COMPOSER: Jennifer Kreisberg
GABRIELINO TRANSLATION AND LANGUAGE COACH: Virginia Carmelo

INTRODUCTION

Tombs of the Vanishing Indian is a work on the cusp. It balances on edges keener than a straight razor and, like the imagery of water and tears the play paints, it rushes at us in a torrent. It is at its inception already a canonical work.

Tombs of the Vanishing Indian lives in between spaces, between our intellect and our emotions, working its way past our constructs and reasoning deeply into our bones. It is a play that upon first reading already insinuates itself along the pathways of our nerves, as it drives itself relentlessly towards the harrowing conclusions that its characters must inevitably face. There is no place for us to escape its breakneck velocity. In its first scene, this dominant theme emerges – flight. Characters running for their lives. The sound of feet running from certain danger. Flashlights. Darkness. And blood mixed with water.

Just as in her earlier work, playwright Marie Clements carves theatrical space to her will. Three sisters. Three spaces. Three glass rooms. Dioramas. Glass cages. Clements, like a surgeon, opens American history unflinchingly. In the life of one family, we see the displacement of communities, the legacy of Indian boarding schools and missions, and finally the forced sterilization programs run by the Indian Health Service and the Bureau of Indian Affairs in the 1950s and 1970s. Andrea Smith, in her 2005 book *Conquest*, examines this attack on women and the government's use of "sexual violence as a tool of genocide." Native women were targeted precisely because their "ability to reproduce continued to [stand] in the way of the [ongoing] conquest of Native lands" (p. 79). In her use of theatrical space, Clements helps us understand that these women's bodies – these vital spaces – are in fact another battlefront for the continuing wars of Manifest Destiny and control.

From the pages of *Tombs of the Vanishing Indian*, the land literally leaps out at the reader, guiding us into knowledge and situating us not so much in a darkened theatre in a northern city but in the deserts of the West. Commissioned in 2003 by Native Voices at the Autry and developed in association with them at the Native Voices at the Autry Playwrights Retreat in Los Angeles in 2004 and 2005, the work is an extension of that community and its sun-drenched landscapes.

Even the language of the land emerges rightfully in Clements's writing. The Gabrielino dialect, brought powerfully into play by the ghost of the three sisters' mother, evokes much more than the culture from which the daughters were taken. It becomes the music of the play, a threnody for an entire generation. But it is easy to look at this use of language in terms of loss of culture – which of the sisters learn it, speak it, once they are cut away from the source? In *Tombs of the Vanishing Indian*, the use of Gabrielino is far more complex. Again, it is one of the means the playwright uses to slip into the in-between spaces of her characters' lives, into the spaces Clements always leaves for her actors to discover. Gabrielino, in the scenes with Detective Fullen, in particular, becomes a shield which The Mother's ghost uses to protect the daughters from the deafening crash of cultures. The Mother says, "Keep me inside of you." The language is what is inside of them, a gift from their mother, and, in theatrical terms, it is the vehicle through which we see their bond come alive onstage.

Of course, Los Angeles, where the play is set, is diverse. Spanish mixes easily with Gabrielino. And the life of the three sisters mixes inevitably with that other culture: Hollywood. Clements delights in opening up the wounds brought about by Hollywood's history, which many indigenous scholars have also explored in recent years. Much of the play's ironic humour emerges from this intersection. Miranda, one of the sisters, remarks to a hack film director, "you wouldn't know dark and mysterious if it licked your behind." Half of the scholarship about Indians on film has just been boiled down to one gleeful sentence.

Clements's potent work will naturally draw comparisons to another play about three sisters. And, yes, there are a few similarities – exquisitely drawn characters, compromised situations, and women searching for something better, but this play is written from the trenches, from the other side of the tracks. It is a clarion cry to rid ourselves of false consciousness and to turn ourselves towards the oncoming flood. This play brings painful knowledge about our collective past but gives us warning to root ourselves in it – to find the shields still embedded therein – or risk being washed away by the deluge.

— MICHAEL GREYEYES

THE LONE WOMAN

Seventy miles off the coast of Los Angeles lies San Nicolas Island, once inhabited by Gabrielino-Tongva Indians. In 1835, a ship arrived to gather the last surviving Indians living there – to take them to Santa Barbara Mission on the mainland. As the ship arrived, a huge storm developed. Fearing the ship was in danger, the captain hurried the Indians on board.

As the ship began to sail, a young Indian mother looked for her baby, who she thought a relative had carried aboard. When she realized her baby was not there, she begged the sailors to turn the ship around … but they would not. She dove overboard to swim to the island and to her baby. Though the waves were large, she managed to reach shore, but never found her baby. She cried for days.

To survive, she built shelter, harvested plants, caught fish, and made fire. She sewed clothing from bird skins. The puppies of wild dogs became her companions. She sang and remembered.

People rumoured that the woman had survived. Several attempts were made to search the island. They found evidence that someone was there. The woman, too, saw the men, but was afraid and hid. Finally, they found her. She smiled, offered them food, and, by hand signs, understood she would go with them to Santa Barbara. Once there, the local Indians did not understand her language.

Many people came to see the woman who had lived eighteen years alone on the island. She was baptized Juana Maria. After just six short weeks, she became ill and died.

She left us her song "Toki Toki," which tells of her contentment on the island but also her longing to leave.

– VIRGINIA CARMELO

STERILIZATION OF NATIVE WOMEN

Sterilization of poor and minority women, including American Indian populations on reserve, was officially sanctioned under the *U.S. Family Planning Act* of 1970. Thousands of poor women and women of colour were sterilized over the next decade, often, according to research by Sally J. Torpy, without full knowledge of the surgical procedure performed on them. U.S. Department of Health, Education, and Welfare records reveal that between 192,000 and 548,000 women were sterilized each year between 1970 and 1977, compared to an average of 63,000 a year between 1907 and 1964, a period which included the zenith of the eugenics movement.

No one even today knows exactly how many Native American women were sterilized during the 1970s. One base for calculation is provided by the U.S. General Accounting Office, whose study covered only four of twelve Indian Health Service regions over four years (1973 through 1976). Within those limits, 3,406 Indian women were sterilized, according to the GAO.

Another estimate is quoted by Bruce E. Johansen at the University of Omaha and provided by Lehman Brightman, who is Lakota, and who devoted much of his life to the issue, suffering a libel suit by doctors in the process. His educated guess (without exact calculations to back it up) is that 40 percent of Native women and 10 percent of Native men were sterilized during the decade. Brightman estimates that the total number of Indian women sterilized during the decade was between 60,000 and 70,000.

RELOCATION PROGRAM

Under the Eisenhower administration elected in 1952, U.S. federal government policy for Native Americans changed towards one of assimilation. One aspect of the assimilation policy was the Relocation Program begun in 1952 and formalized under the *Indian Relocation Act* of 1956. This program encouraged young Native Americans to leave reservations by offering one-way bus fare to the city and the promise of assistance finding jobs, housing, and vocational training there. In 1940, 13 percent of Indians lived in urban areas, but by 1980 more than half were urban, according to James Olson in *Native Americans in the Twentieth Century* (1984, p. 163). The Bureau of Indian Affairs estimates that 200,000 Indians were relocated, whereas the *Indian Removal Act* of 1830 forced fewer than half this number (89,000) to relocate. The relocation policy continued until 1962 and the election of Kennedy and Democratic administrations. The Relocation Program was formally discontinued in 1972.

TOMBS OF THE VANISHING INDIAN

CAST

THE WOMEN

JESSIE: A striking woman, smart and capable but bound. Indian, age twenty-seven.

MIRANDA: A beautiful Hollywood star–wannabe. Naive but tough minded and strong willed. Indian, age twenty-five.

JANEY: A young, delicately beautiful street woman. Fragile but tough. Indian, age twenty-one.

THE MOTHER: Also plays THE LONE WOMAN, fifty-five-year-old Gabrielino woman from the 1800s; RUTH, Jewish-Indian patient, age forty-five; and SARAH, an Indian patient, age eighteen.

THE BLACKCOATS

DR. DANIEL HANSEN: Jessie's older doctor husband. Good looking and logical, in control of his room. White, age thirty-nine. Also plays BLACKCOAT THREE.

BOB STILLS: A very stereotypical Hollywood director. Once considered golden, he has seen better days. White, age forty-five. Also plays BLACKCOAT TWO and WHITE INTERN ONE.

DETECTIVE FULLEN: A detective who is quirky but intelligent and compassionate. White, age forty-seven. Also plays BLACKCOAT ONE and WHITE INTERN TWO.

SETTING

TIME AND PLACE

PAST: 1955, Los Angeles
PRESENT: 1973, Los Angeles

DIORAMA STAGE SET

The space is quite open and curved to show the backdrops of each woman's Indian Room – rich painting-like scenarios that are activated by the drama in each room. Each woman's Indian Room is decorated like set pieces in the diorama of a museum. They are incredibly familiar but fake.

The backdrops in each Indian Room fade in layers in a modern treatment of the Daguerre Dioramas shown in Paris in the 1820s. The domestic lighting is reflective of an exhibit – hard edged and stark – but lighting on the diorama backdrops is controlled between media layers so that they deepen into three dimensions.

Finally, each woman's Indian Room is encased in glass as if history is animating before the audience, untouchable, until the glass is broken and their stories are no longer separate or containable.

Inside a structured darkness, the voice of THE LONE WOMAN penetrates the space, growing louder, calling out from nothing as drums begin to beat, and a thousand Indian women's voices reach each other and echo down a long tunnel.

At the opening of the tunnel a light reveals the shadows of THE MOTHER and her three daughters, standing. THE MOTHER picks up JANEY, age three, and grabs the hand of MIRANDA, age seven, who grabs the hand of JESSIE, age nine. They move into the tunnel, beginning to run inside, their breath echoing, their feet splashing down in streams of water.

They stop in the middle of a crossroads where the tunnel branches out into three possibilities. They stop as THE MOTHER bends down to whisper to them.

THE MOTHER
You have to promise me ... Miranda, look at me when I talk to you.

MIRANDA
Yes, Momma ...

THE MOTHER
Jessie, hold Momma's hand ... Remember my hands, Jessie.

JESSIE
Yes, Momma ...

THE MOTHER
They are going to come for me ... but they are going to take you ... that's what they do ... Now hold Janey. Hold her tight, Jessie ... Shhh, baby ... my baby Janey. My babies ...

THE MOTHER bends down and kisses JANEY, and then grabs the faces of her daughters, kissing them, beginning to cry as lights from three flashlights scan the space and the large shadows of THREE BLACKCOATS begin to close in.

THE MOTHER
You have to promise me you will run …

MIRANDA and JESSIE
Yes, Momma …

THE MOTHER
Keep me inside … Deep inside so they can't take me away from you …

MIRANDA and JESSIE
Yes, Momma.

THE MOTHER
Momma loves you … loves you so much.

> *THE BLACKCOATS approach, their footsteps getting closer and closer.*

When I say run … run and if they catch you … keep me inside … whatever happens, keep me deep inside. Remember there are three of you, you will always survive … You are a part of something bigger … you are mine.

> *A flashlight beam hits THE MOTHER's face.*

BLACKCOAT ONE
I see them. Right over here …

> *She pushes her daughters behind her as the giant shadows of the THREE BLACKCOATS approach.*

THE MOTHER
Get away … get away, Takers /

BLACKCOAT TWO
/ Damn Indians …

THE MOTHER

Do you hear me? … / You are going to have to kill me to get them … / They are mine … They are mine.

BLACKCOAT ONE

/ Ma'am, you are gonna have to calm down. You know you're not supposed to be here …

BLACKCOAT THREE

/ Probably doesn't understand American …

BLACKCOAT ONE

/ Moron …

THE MOTHER

Get away … / get away, Takers …

BLACKCOAT THREE

/ I meant English … / you know what I mean …

THE MOTHER

/ I want you to have … I want …

> *THE MOTHER puts her hand in her dress pocket and raises her hand to give it to JESSIE.*

BLACKCOAT TWO

/ Dammit … / She's got a gun …

JESSIE

Here, Jessie … / take the rock …

BLACKCOAT ONE

/ I don't think …

> *BLACKCOAT THREE raises his gun.*
>
> *SFX: The sound of a gun blast that echoes.*
>
> *THE MOTHER falls back from the blast and into the stream dead. Her three daughters, JESSIE, MIRANDA, and JANEY, look down at her in shock as their shadows get larger, shaped like three women's shadows.*

JESSIE bends down to her mother and picks up the rock clenched in her hand.

JESSIE

Her blood is mixing with the river around our feet, and suddenly her silencing came just like she said it would. Just like she said …

THE MOTHER

(*voiceover*) Run.

> *SFX: The sound of three sets of young feet running down three tunnels.*

> *SFX: The sound of crying.*

MIRANDA

Except now there is screaming in three directions all the way down the long tunnel and into the painful light.

> *They stand frozen as THE MOTHER disappears.*

JANEY

She is gone, our centre is gone, and like a triangle we descend into the vanishing.

> *Fade to black.*

> *The space carves itself into three separate rooms encased by glass. Lights up on each room, animating each story.*

∼ *Janey's Indian Room*

> *JANEY, age twenty-one, stands dishevelled and dirty in the middle of a Los Angeles jail interview room. DETECTIVE FULLEN sits looking over a file. There is one door, one table, two chairs, and seemingly no windows. DETECTIVE FULLEN suddenly looks up.*

DETECTIVE FULLEN

The report says your name is Juana Maria.

> *JANEY doesn't respond but looks out into the glass.*

THE LONE WOMAN

(*offstage, Gabrielino*) Maxaatneme netwaanyano. 'aawte' xaa, xaayne hyoonax. Menee' netwaanyan, Juana Maria, maayot nenuuno nooma'.

> *SUBTITLE (text)*
>> My name was given to me. How true it is, I don't know. This – my name, Juana Maria – has made me alone.

> *JANEY hears the voice and looks in the room and then around the space. DETECTIVE FULLEN watches JANEY while taking down notes.*

DETECTIVE FULLEN

Would it be better if I talked to you in Spanish?

> *He smiles at JANEY, inviting a response. She looks up, searching for the voice.*

It wouldn't be better for me because I don't speak Spanish … stupid, I know …

> *Pause.*

> *Hoping for a response, DETECTIVE FULLEN stares at JANEY.*

Excellent. Why don't we start again … My name is Detective Charles Fullen … the third … if we are going to be formal.

> *He holds out his hand to JANEY.*

THE LONE WOMAN

(*offstage, Gabrielino*) Paahe'ha'av xaa?

> *SUBTITLE (text)*
>> There are three of you?

> *JANEY smiles at the voice. DETECTIVE FULLEN smiles at JANEY uncomfortably.*

DETECTIVE FULLEN

There are three of me. Not literally of course. My grandfather, my father, and then me … What can I say … great things come in threes …

> *Suddenly, JANEY talks.*

JANEY

> (*Spanish*) O gran tragedia.

DETECTIVE FULLEN

> Great tragedies ... I got that one ...
>
>> *He gets excited as if he is getting somewhere.*
>
> While we're on a roll ... Do you know the date today? Why you are being kept here?
>
>> *The image of THE LONE WOMAN appears as a reflection in the glass. She is a beautiful Gabrielino Indian, age fifty-five, dressed in a long skirt and a scarf that wraps around her in layers.*

THE LONE WOMAN

> (*Gabrielino*) Weheesh mahaar koy weheesh wachaa' koy mahareesh weheesh mahaar koy paahe', Santa Barbara Mission.
>
>> *SUBTITLE (text)*
>> 1853. Santa Barbara Mission.
>
>> *JANEY turns towards the voice.*

JANEY

> 1973. Los Angeles.
>
>> *They look at each other.*

THE LONE WOMAN

> (*Gabrielino*) Pariitshmenokreme 'eyoomom, eyoomtaax ng'aro.
>
>> *SUBTITLE (text)*
>> They should have left us to our own.

JANEY

> (*Spanish*) Si.

DETECTIVE FULLEN

> *Si* ... *Si* ... Yes. What? *Qué?* Shit ...
>
>> *JANEY nods.*

JANEY
   I know you now. I know your reflection.

THE LONE WOMAN
   (*Gabrielino*) Yaraarkomokre neshuunnga.

>   *SUBTITLE (text)*
>   I remember you in my heart.

DETECTIVE FULLEN
   Juana … look at me.

>   *He takes in her blood-stained dress and strange behaviour
>   and softens.*

   Look, I'm sorry that no one has been here to look after your physical,
   or ment– … needs. There was … is a huge backup as usual … a real
   zoo … Maybe we should just start again … Why don't you take a seat?

>   *JANEY looks up as the fluorescent lights begin to flutter. She
>   looks out at the glass as a landscape begins to reflect back …*

   You're mad at the zoo comment … I didn't mean that in any
   derogatory way … it's a common phrase … a saying …

>   *A shoreline and shifting sands blow and swirl around THE
>   LONE WOMAN.*

>   *THE LONE WOMAN begins to speak and JANEY, connected
>   to her, begins to translate her language and story, shifting
>   the language from Gabrielino to Spanish, creating an
>   understanding between them that the English subtitles
>   document.*

JANEY
   (*Spanish*) Ella diría / era un día caluroso sin aliento, y luego el viento
   empezó a soplar en todas las direcciones haciendo que la arena escale
   el aire. Se tallo los ojos, y luego allí estaban … como tú con sus abrigos
   negros. Áspero en sus ojos.

>   *SUBTITLE (text)*
>   She would say /

THE LONE WOMAN

(*Gabrielino*) Mexaaxshmenokne, oroo tamta xaroot, xaay ahiiken. Koy yeekaw, chataakmok'e puu ahiiken 'wee yoyooxarenga, 'Ohweet'e maaynok 'epeekmok ahiikeng'aro. Naxyaatne nechoochona, koy yeekaw, Omoom'e xaroot koy mokoochan yomaaxa. Ataamchin nechoochonga.

> SUBTITLE (*text*)
>
> I would say it was a hot day, without breath. And then the wind began to blow in all directions. Making the sand go up into the air. I rubbed my eyes, and then – there you were with your black coats. Coarse in my eyes.

DETECTIVE FULLEN desperately tries to keep up to JANEY with his Spanish–English translation book.

DETECTIVE FULLEN

Ella diría? Who would say? *Día caluroso … viento …* wind … *arena …* sand … *sus ojos …* her eyes … *allí estaban …* Who was there? *Áspero en sus ojos …* coarse in her eyes … I think … we … are getting confused with the differences in … languages … Shit.

JANEY

(*Spanish*) Mierda.

> *THE LONE WOMAN looks at JANEY and smiles.*

THE LONE WOMAN

(*Gabrielino*) Menee'e xariiy yaawk 'ayoo'em totomoomoyt.

> SUBTITLE (*text*)
>
> This place – has many difficulties.

DETECTIVE FULLEN

I just want a straight answer to a straight question, preferably in English.

> *DETECTIVE FULLEN rewinds the tape recorder on the table.*
>
> *SFX: The sound of the tape rolling backwards and then clunking.*

Maybe this will help. Do you remember this?

THE LONE WOMAN
(*Gabrielino*) Xaayne yaawk chinuuho'a.

> *SUBTITLE (text)*
> I have no baby.

> *He pushes Play.*

> *SFX: The sound of JANEY crying hysterically rolls forward.*

> *THE LONE WOMAN closes her eyes as tears roll down her face. She begins to softly sing, keen, under the following scene.*

JANEY
(*voiceover*) Please, I want my baby. I want my baby back. Please. God, please ... I want my baby back ...

DETECTIVE FULLEN
(*voiceover*) Where is your baby? Juana ... tell us where your baby is and we'll go and get it ...

JANEY
(*voiceover*) My baby ... My baby is dead ... my baby is dead ... because of me ... my baby is dead ... it's my fault ... my fault ...

> *DETECTIVE FULLEN shuts off the tape recorder.*

DETECTIVE FULLEN
Do you remember saying this, Juana? Do you remember being on the streets, being picked up, your dress and hands bloody? They think you murdered your baby and they are searching every alley in the vicinity until they find his body. Do you understand? I'd like to tell them different. Talk to me. Let's cut the bullshit. You speak English ... you understand what's going on here ...

> *JANEY slowly looks at THE LONE WOMAN, who shakes her head but says nothing. JANEY looks coldly at DETECTIVE FULLEN.*

JANEY
(*Spanish*) No hablo inglés.

> *Lights fade.*

From the other side of a pane of glass, JESSIE, age twenty-seven, sits at a desk in a doctor's office that is furnished in white. She sets THE MOTHER's rock down on the edge of the desk. It stares back at her. JESSIE clears her throat as if beginning something important.

JESSIE

Hello, my name is Dr. Hansen, and I am your doctor. Your name, please?

She nods, listening to an unvoiced answer.

Mr. Rock ... I see ... how fitting. As I was saying, "How are you, Mr. Rock, and what brings you to our clinic?"

She listens.

I see, you have no money, but pain. No, no, no worries, that's why we are here ... to help penniless pain.

She observes his shape.

It looks like you've lost your edge ... you've become round.

She listens.

You were travelling out West from Oklahoma to L.A. to start a new life. How did you come?

She smiles.

You rolled. I can see why you might be in pain.

She picks up the rock.

I dreamed once I had a mother and she had me, and I had two sisters, and she had them, and we were on a bus, with a skinny grey dog on the side, and my younger sister barfed on the floor, and it smelled, and my other sister buried her baby face in my mother's deep breast and drank like that river was hers. I dreamed once I had a mother and she had me and I had two sisters and she had them and we were on a bus with a skinny grey dog on the side, and we were travelling a long way to make a new story, and it was hot and my mother opened the bus window, and a beautiful stream of wind came over us and it blew my mother's black hair all over our round faces, which lay on my mother's body like we owned her. She said just then, "Look, girls, look at those rocks." These three big boulders standing just so in the desert, staring just enough for us to recognize them. She said, "Jessie, look. Don't you recognize them from home? Look how they stand," and I said, "Yes, I think I do." She said, "Jessie, the rock family is following us to L.A., to start a new life too." Such are the things memories are made of.

Her husband, DR. DANIEL HANSEN, appears behind her wearing a dark suit. He nuzzles into her ear.

DANIEL
Jessie ...

JESSIE
Sorry ... I was just getting my head together /

DANIEL
/ by talking to a rock. You're lucky I'm not jealous.

JESSIE
Well, he listens to me. Plus ... he's always hard.

DANIEL
A perfect man, I suppose. Well, tell him to take it easy because you're mine ... God, I've missed you. Six months is a long time ...

JESSIE
We did it ... we got through being apart ... I'm glad you took this posting even if you had to come out West earlier than me ... live in the sun ... get a tan ...

DANIEL
Hey ... I've been working my butt off ...

JESSIE
Let's see ...

He shows his butt; she looks at it.

DANIEL
You shouldn't be looking at the Senior Attending's butt ... at least not on the first day of work.

JESSIE

Who's going to report me?

DANIEL

You got me …

He gets serious, moving towards her.

We made the right decision to practise here … I know Los Angeles wasn't your first choice … but I think we can make a real difference to people who really deserve a chance … we're working together just like we always planned.

She smiles at him lovingly.

JESSIE

You know what I love about you?

DANIEL

I'm good looking and …

JESSIE

No … yes … but you always surprise me.

He draws her closer.

DANIEL

I think you love me because I let you talk to things that aren't alive.

She looks at her rock.

JESSIE

Don't talk that way about my rock.

They embrace.

He says nice things about you.

DANIEL

I doubt it.

JESSIE

I say nice things about you to him.

DANIEL

Like what?

JESSIE

Like I love you, Dr. Hansen.

DANIEL

I love you too … Dr. Hansen.

Lights fade.

⌒ *Miranda's Indian Room*

From the other side of a pane of glass, MIRANDA, age twenty-five, stands holding a film script in her hand. Across the room, BOB STILLS, feeling the part of the director, looks at her with meaning.

BOB STILLS

This is a western. What does that mean to you?

MIRANDA

It means Indians die.

BOB STILLS

That's all you got out of it reading it.

MIRANDA

Pretty much.

He squints and leans back, looking at her.

Do you want me to read the lines?

BOB STILLS puffs up to inform.

BOB STILLS

I think we owe them more than that, don't you? How much do you know about Indians, Miss Miranda?

MIRANDA

I know I *am* an Indian.

He looks up at her speechless and then down at his papers.

BOB STILLS

You *are*? You are. I'm sorry, I didn't know you were Indian. Casting should have written that down somewhere.

MIRANDA

Well, it's true … Do you want me to read the lines?

BOB STILLS

I'm sorry, I thought you were … oh … I don't know. I didn't think
that far. I thought you were dark … and I'm looking for dark … and
mysterious.

She smiles, trying to get the job despite herself.

MIRANDA

You've come to the right place.

BOB STILLS

I don't know if I feel comfortable with an Indian reading for an
Indian …

She looks at him. Steps closer to coddle him, and then speaks.

MIRANDA

(*pissed off*) Oh … fuck it. You don't have to finish, it's all bullshit
anyway … You wouldn't know dark and mysterious if it licked your
behind.

She turns to leave.

BOB STILLS

What did you say?

She stops.

MIRANDA

It's an old Apache proverb.

BOB STILLS

How does it go?

She turns and looks directly at him.

MIRANDA

I don't know. I just made it up.

BOB STILLS

Do you want the part … or not?

Pause.

MIRANDA

What's the catch?

Pause.

BOB STILLS

No catch … It's a supporting role. Three pages. Three lines.

He smiles.

Not bad for your first time out.

She smiles.

MIRANDA

Not bad.

BOB STILLS

You get shot … is that going to cause you any pain?

MIRANDA

No, we're pretty used to being shot.

He pauses and smiles.

BOB STILLS

It's just make-believe. That's what our business is here. Make-believe.

She approaches him.

MIRANDA

Hmm … I wonder where all the spirits of dead Indians go when they've been shot in the movies.

BOB STILLS

What?

MIRANDA

If it's our business to make people believe, then don't you think they think it's true, and, if they think it's true, don't you think it becomes real, somewhere down the line.

BOB STILLS

I'm not following /

MIRANDA

/ Does it become real for them, the people you are making the movie for … I mean if you keep seeing an Indian get shot and die, get shot and die, get shot and die /

BOB STILLS

/ I get the point.

MIRANDA

Do you?

She stops in front of him.

BOB STILLS

I don't know … You know … you make my head hurt …

He stands up.

Did you see *Little Big Man*?

She smiles.

MIRANDA

Yes.

BOB STILLS

Then let's just say, "Come out and fight … it is a good day to die."

He puts his hand out. She shakes it. Lights fade.

⌒ *Janey's Indian Room*

DETECTIVE FULLEN stands looking at JANEY from a distance. JANEY looks only at THE LONE WOMAN, who is holding a baby wrapped in blankets. She leans down and puts the baby in JANEY's arms.

JANEY

He is beautiful.

She touches the baby's small face.

You have to pretend there is hope when they are in your arms, don't you?

She stops and tears form in her eyes.

When I am alone, there is just a tomb in the pit of my belly where the thought of him used to be.

She looks down at the baby.

Here now this child is in my arms, at my nipple, on my lap, in my hair; here he is in my mouth, in my eyes, just like I remembered.

She holds his little fist.

Baby. Sweet brown. Here, I am a home with a child in it.

THE LONE WOMAN

(*Gabrielino*) Mohaay xaa akkeehan takwiinok, nemaamanme takwiinok xaa mohaay ma'eete'.

> *SUBTITLE (text)*
> An empty womb is bad, my empty arms are bad.

DETECTIVE FULLEN moves towards JANEY.

(*Gabrielino*) Hyoonaxme 'ooma', taarxen hyoonax 'a 'ook.

> *SUBTITLE (text)*
> He knows you, a child knows his mother.

THE LONE WOMAN begins to move away as DETECTIVE FULLEN approaches.

JANEY

Please stay.

THE LONE WOMAN looks at DETECTIVE FULLEN.

THE LONE WOMAN

(*Gabrielino*) Pomoo shiraaw'ax xaa nanowre.

> *SUBTITLE (text)*
> Their speaking is dull.

In a series of fades, THE LONE WOMAN walks across the shifting sands of her island. JANEY begins to sing to the baby as DETECTIVE FULLEN pulls a chair close to her.

DETECTIVE FULLEN

You're not going to talk to me, are you? Busy there with what it seems like … it's a baby … is it your baby, Juana?

No response.

I know you can hear me.

He listens to her singing.

The song is not Mexican is it? Because you are not Mexican. You are Indian, aren't you? And this is an Indian song … it's beautiful.

He looks at her and decides to talk if she won't.

It reminds me of a room … a room in my grandfather's house. He called it his Indian Room and he collected all sorts of Indian things – baskets and regalia, arrowheads, weapons and carving tools …

He looks at the room they are in.

You must feel like you have been collected. It must make you feel scared … Are you scared, Juana?

She looks at him briefly.

I'll tell you a secret. I loved that room. It's old fashioned but I loved it … I loved it and … I was scared of it. Not their things so much … but the violence I felt in that room … There's violence in this room too, isn't there?

She ignores him but is listening.

Do you want to know what scared me the most? I was scared that all the Indians my grandfather took from were hiding under the sofa, or under a chair – in the corners of darkness I couldn't see. That they were just waiting to come back for what was theirs … and when they came they would think I had something to do with it … AND they would scalp my little blond head …

A beautiful trickle of laughter falls from her mouth. He looks at her warmly and smiles.

You think that's funny, don't you … well, at least you laughed.

Lights fade.

⌒ *Jessie's Indian Room*

> *JESSIE stands behind an examining table. A white sheet*
> *creates a teepee-like shape over a woman's legs in stirrups.*

JESSIE

I'm sorry, you're going to have to open a bit wider. That's it ... it won't take long.

> *JESSIE fumbles with her tools.*

There's nothing to be nervous about.

RUTH

I'm not nervous. You're nervous.

JESSIE

Okay. I'm nervous.

RUTH

I had six children ... nothing about spreading my legs makes me nervous anymore ... so you can relax.

JESSIE

Thank you. I think ... You didn't have any records ... and it makes sense we do a complete physical. Have you been to this clinic before?

RUTH

No.

JESSIE

Is there somewhere we can phone and get your records?

RUTH

No phone. No records. Is there something wrong down there?

JESSIE

No ... I mean ... I'm just trying to put a file together for you so next time you can come in and we know who you are – your medical history and so on ...

RUTH

That's reassuring.

RUTH looks up from behind the tent for a moment.

RUTH
You Indian?

Taken aback by the question, JESSIE tries to answer honestly.

JESSIE
No … I mean yes … but not really. I was adopted and raised by a Caucasian couple …

RUTH
Caucasian. Sounds like a flower. A delicate white flower.

JESSIE
Sure … I guess.

RUTH
You a real doctor?

JESSIE
Yes.

RUTH
That's a dangerous combination. A real, educated Indian woman.

JESSIE
I wouldn't call myself an Indian woman.

RUTH
Why … they take that away from you too?

JESSIE pauses.

JESSIE
You can get dressed now …

JESSIE rises from the stool and turns with her tray.

She begins to clean her tools as RUTH rises – a beautiful, older Indian woman whose naked body is proud with the scars of motherhood. She dresses slowly, comfortable in her nakedness. JESSIE looks down at her chart and then uncomfortably fiddles with the tools on the tray.

We'll run these tests but you are in pretty good health … except for your tonsils, which are inflamed and probably should have been taken out a long time ago … I'm going to refer you to Dr. Hansen …

> RUTH *looks at her.*

The other Dr. Hansen … and we can set you up an appointment next week, to come in and have them removed.

RUTH

Is removal always the answer?

JESSIE

If you want something permanently resolved … yes, it is …

RUTH

You like your tools?

JESSIE

That's how I make my living.

RUTH

The Gabrielinos probably would have said that's how they make things live. They were a Native American tribe here …

JESSIE

I didn't know that.

RUTH

As a practice, you should always know whose land you're walking on.

JESSIE

Like I said … I wasn't brought up Indian …

RUTH

Not to worry … it will catch up with you.

> JESSIE *looks at her uncomfortably.*

Those Gabrielinos loved their tools too … they believed that the tools they worked with had their own spirits … funny, huh? … So when they died their loved ones would have to kill their tools so that they could join them in the spirit world.

JESSIE

How do you know that?

RUTH

I know my own stories … I'm part Gabrielino Indian … part Jewish …

They look at each other eye to eye.

Sometimes history is too painful to remember, but we remember anyways because we are still working it out, aren't we?

Lights fade.

∼ *Miranda's Indian Room*

From the darkness of MIRANDA'S INDIAN ROOM.

SFX: The sound of a snappy scene marker.

Lights up.

BOB STILLS

(*offstage*) ACTION!

SFX: The sound of a gun blast.

Lights up on MIRANDA dressed as an Indian princess on a western movie set. She begins the long process of dying, and goes this way and that, making the most of her big moment. First shock, then fear, then acceptance and, finally, as Indian princess …

MIRANDA

I am dying. It is a good day to die … As usual.

She finally collapses full on the earth, hand raised for one last goodbye. BOB STILLS paces impatiently.

BOB STILLS

(*screams*) CUT!

He braces himself.

Miss Miranda … Breathtaking … I have never seen anything quite like it before … except …

He puts his hand on her shoulder.

... for a few minor details. This is a small part ... what we call a bit part ... YOU are not the star –

He points offstage, suggesting that he is pointing to a white genteel lady who is smiling with a cowboy in a white Stetson.

– the genteel lady with the parasol is the STAR – and the guy with the white cowboy hat is the leading man.

He looks back at her.

Get it?

MIRANDA
Got it.

He begins to walk away but, making a show, comes back ...

BOB STILLS
Oh ... one small thing ... The lines as I have in my script read "I am dying. It is a good day to die ... Ash, ooal," which translates in English to "Farewell, we will see each other again."

He looks at her.

Do we need that translation again ... or do you have it?

MIRANDA
"Ash, ooal" ... means "Farewell, we will see each other again"? Wild ... okay ... No ... It's good. I got it. Really.

Grandly, he begins to walk back.

BOB STILLS
Let's go from the top again, all right?

She begins to walk back to her mark, mumbling under her breath.

MIRANDA
It does sound like "as usual" to me ... but, hey ...

Hearing her, BOB STILLS stops and turns.

... I'm just a bit actor here. Indian background ...

BOB STILLS
Are you getting political on my set?

She turns to look at him.

MIRANDA

No, just kidding … geez … sorry … okay … I'm psyched!

BOB STILLS nods his head. She gathers her inner Indian princess.

SFX: The sound of snappy scene marker.

BOB STILLS

Rolling … ACTION!

SFX: The sound of a gun blast.

MIRANDA, the Indian princess, begins the short and precise process of dying again, almost bored.

MIRANDA

I am dying. It is a good day to die … Ash … ooal.

BOB STILLS

Cut!

MIRANDA

What! I said ash … ooal.

BOB STILLS

That's not it. It was good but do you think you could put a little more feeling into it?

She turns her head.

MIRANDA

Asshole.

BOB STILLS

It's ass-ooal.

BOB STILLS looks at her with a small smile.

MIRANDA

That's what I said.

She looks back at him sweetly.

BOB STILLS
That's what I thought you said.

Lights fade.

⌒ *Janey's Indian Room*

> *In a series of fades, THE LONE WOMAN stands on the <u>shore of her island</u>. She looks down at JANEY and the baby.*

THE LONE WOMAN
(*Gabrielino*) Peshiinar're xaa woshaa'ax. Wii'a hoohowaraweesh mopiinng'aro koy eyootaarxen. Paa'ro meheepko paxaayt xaa ashuunnga 'ooma'.

> SUBTITLE (*text*)
> The Taker is looking at us. Pull the dream to your breast and our child. Drink while there is a river left inside you.

> *JANEY looks down and into the face of her baby. She opens her dress and places his face next her to breast.*

JANEY
Do you still miss even the thought of him?

> *She looks down at the mother and child.*

THE LONE WOMAN
(*Gabrielino*) Schmehokne tataamet xaroot 'wee tehoovet. Hunuuko' xaroot 'wee tee'e. Hawtok hamaare.

> SUBTITLE (*text*)
> They were gone from the beginning.

> *JANEY smiles down at his thirst.*

JANEY
They are so alive … so thirsty for life … how can they ever be gone?

> *She looks at JANEY as if realizing it herself.*

THE LONE WOMAN
(*Gabrielino*) Schmehokne tataamet xaroot 'wee tehoovet. Hunuuko' xaroot 'wee tee'e. Hawtok hamaare. Hyaane mokaanax koy hyaa'ra'

mokaanax mo'iikok. ooma"a toi't xaa. Hoohowaraweeshve sakaape'
taamet.

> SUBTITLE (*text*)
>> They are gone from the beginning. I killed him and you
>> killed your son … just by conceiving of him. From a dream
>> of a brighter day.

> *JANEY holds the baby desperately to her.*

JANEY

I don't want to know what you are talking about … I don't want to
talk about this … I don't want to think about it … Please just let me be
with him …

THE LONE WOMAN

(*Gabrielino*) Kimaame.

> SUBTITLE (*text*)
>> They are coming.

> *JANEY holds the baby tighter.*

JANEY

No …

THE LONE WOMAN

(*Gabrielino*) Yaawk'aa momwaa ashuung'aro. Yaawk'aa'ra momwaa
'ashuunng' aro, 'ashuunng'aro. Waraak'e ashuunnga xaa, 'anaange xaare
pomoo'ook.

> SUBTITLE (*text*)
>> Hold him inside. Hold him very close inside, inside. It is only
>> from the inside, we are still mothers.

> *SFX: The sound of a door buzzer.*

> *JANEY frantically turns and looks as the door begins to
> open and then back down at her suddenly babyless arms.*

JANEY

You've made me lose my baby … see what you have done?

DETECTIVE FULLEN

Juana, what's wrong?

> *She begins to search the floor on her hands and knees.*
> *DETECTIVE FULLEN motions to TWO WHITE INTERNS.*
> *They move around her.*

THE LONE WOMAN

(*Gabrielino*) 'Ekweeschmenokne nechinuuho'a.

> SUBTITLE (*text*)
> I want to take care of my baby.

JANEY

He's gone … he's gone … He was right here … no … no … Where are you? Where are you? He's got to be here somewhere … he couldn't have gone far …

DETECTIVE FULLEN

He's not here, Juana … your baby's not here … he never was …

JANEY

Liar.

> *She stops and finally sees the TWO WHITE INTERNS.*

DETECTIVE FULLEN

They're just going to take you to a doctor. Get you checked out and cleaned up …

> *JANEY begins to back away from him.*

JANEY

No … Why are you doing this? Why? I didn't do anything to you. Why can't you just leave me alone?

THE LONE WOMAN

(*Gabrielino*) Xaayre' hamiingko' nongiinok 'eyooma' eyoonuuno?

> SUBTITLE (*text*)
> Why can't you leave us alone? /

JANEY

/ <u>Why can't you just leave us alone to lo</u>ve.

> *DETECTIVE FULLEN and the TWO WHITE INTERNS
> slowly move towards her as she backs away.*

DETECTIVE FULLEN

It's for your own good, Juana … you'll feel better … I promise …

JANEY

Get away from me … get away from me … I know your hands … I know what your hands do …

DETECTIVE FULLEN

Please don't make this any harder than it has to be … look at me … look at me …

> *DETECTIVE FULLEN grabs her face and the TWO WHITE
> INTERNS grab her. She looks at him with hatred.*

JANEY

Fuck you … fuck you and your promises …

> *They pick her up and begin to haul her out of the room.*
>
> *Lights fade.*

〜 Jessie's Indian Room

> *JESSIE and DANIEL enter their 1970s apartment. It is sparse
> and carefully decorated. They enter in a rush, arguing and
> undoing their well-put-together dinner clothes throughout.*

DANIEL

… It wasn't that bad …

JESSIE

For you.

DANIEL

Okay … I'm sorry … it was pretty embarrassing … he's just got a weird sense of humour.

JESSIE

So you thought his comment was funny …

DANIEL

No … I didn't think it was funny … he was *trying* to be / funny …

JESSIE

/ It's racist.

DANIEL

So you're calling the representative for the Indian Health Service racist?

> *DANIEL stops.*

Okay … why don't we just calm down …

JESSIE

Why don't *you* calm down?

DANIEL

I am calm … I'm just trying to understand why you're so upset …

JESSIE

Really? You have to *try* to understand /

DANIEL

/ I just don't get it. You never want to talk about your past but you have no problem cutting people in half when they bring up anything to do with Indianness.

JESSIE

That's not fair. I just don't like pompous assholes who spout out falsehoods as if they are the authority.

DANIEL

All he said was, "What do you think of the theory that Indians can't handle their liquor?"

JESSIE

Think about it … Why do you think he said that? He said that because his poodle wife said, "Dear, I've been looking at you and I can't lay my finger on what you are? Indian? Well, isn't that ironic?" Whatever that means … He said that so I could be put in some place he feels superior …

DANIEL

That doesn't warrant your response.

JESSIE

I just told him the truth. That there is no scientific evidence to back up his "theory," but while we were on the subject the truth is that the white man gave Indians alcohol and the Indian gave the white man tobacco … and it's hard to tell who's ahead. He didn't have much to say after that.

DANIEL

That's because he was choking on his cigar.

JESSIE

Wishful thinking …

> *He stops and reprimands her.*

DANIEL

Jessie … I hate it when you get this way … You have to learn to /

JESSIE

/ Learn to what?

DANIEL

Not be so emotional. Think before you speak.

JESSIE

Or just not talk … that would be easier …

DANIEL

I didn't say that.

> *DANIEL approaches her. She moves from him slightly. He spits it out.*

It's just that I have to report to this guy … most of our patients are Indian … which means a lot of paper for me.

> *He opens up a cabinet, takes out a bottle of scotch and a glass, and begins to pour.*

JESSIE
You have to report to him ... for what?

DANIEL
Statistics ...

He turns and takes a drink.

JESSIE
That's it?

DANIEL
What's wrong? We don't have to go out with him, them, again ... okay?
I thought it might be nice to meet another couple and go out to dinner
like normal people.

Silence. He tries again.

Can we end this?

JESSIE
Sure ... Do you like how I said that?

He smiles.

DANIEL
Impressive ... It's being here in Los Angeles, isn't it?

She doesn't look at him.

JESSIE
What do you mean?

DANIEL
Why don't you try and find your sisters now that we're here. I can help.

JESSIE
I've searched for years, Daniel. They're nowhere to be found. It's as if
they didn't even exist. Or I don't.

He smells her.

DANIEL
I see you.

JESSIE
Do you?

Lights fade.

∼ *Miranda's Indian Room*

MIRANDA clicks on the light to reveal the dressing room of a western movie set. She hears a noise in the closet and picks up a prop tomahawk.

MIRANDA
Hello … is anybody there? I know you're there. I can hear you breathing, or should I say I can hear you stumbling …

From behind a closet the muffled voice of BOB STILLS.

BOB STILLS
Fuckin' … small closet.

MIRANDA
If you don't come out from that closet, I'm going to scream; which I can do really well, because I'm a trained actress, an Indian, and I have a tomahawk. That's a triple threat.

BOB STILLS
It's just me.

MIRANDA
Sure, it is.

BOB STILLS
Seriously, it's me.

MIRANDA
Me who?

BOB STILLS
Bob.

MIRANDA
Bob?

BOB STILLS

Mr. Stills … Mr. Stills … Bob … Stills. I left something in here, and then I heard footsteps and it was too late to get out so I just shut the door.

MIRANDA

Weird. Why don't you come out now?

BOB STILLS

I can't.

MIRANDA

Why not?

BOB STILLS

Trust me. I can't.

He waits for her response. Nothing.

It's a long story. I was looking for a place to relax so I came down to the costume department.

MIRANDA

So why don't you come out?

BOB STILLS

It's embarrassing.

MIRANDA

Come out anyways …

BOB STILLS

You wouldn't understand.

MIRANDA

Try me.

BOB STILLS

Trust me, you wouldn't. Are you going to leave?

MIRANDA

No … not on your life.

He walks out in full Indian buckskin.

BOB STILLS

Jesus, then take a good, long look …

His hands cross in front of his air-conditioned crotch.

Fuuuck … Satisfied.

She begins to laugh uncontrollably as BOB STILLS stands in full buckskin regalia.

MIRANDA

The question is … Are you satisfied?

BOB STILLS

Very funny … Very fuckin' funny here … I just wanted to try it out. Okay … I was feelin' down, which I might add you are not helping, and I got to thinking about when I was a kid, and how great it was to play Cowboys and Indians. It made me happy. Simpler times … you know …

MIRANDA

Let me guess … you always played the Indian.

BOB STILLS

My secret's out. I might as well just come clean … Do you want to smoke a joint?

MIRANDA

How! Big Chief want to smoke peace pipe.

BOB STILLS

Fuck … what do I care? Don't smoke, smoke, but I need to relax.

He rolls a joint.

MIRANDA

You think just dressing like an Indian would help you relax. But hey, you look good. Seriously. Sorta. A well-put-together white guy in buckskin … Okay … this is fucked up.

BOB STILLS

That's Hollywood.

MIRANDA
Is that your answer to everything?

BOB STILLS
When I can get away with it. What about you?

MIRANDA
What about me?

BOB STILLS
You ever play Cowboys and Indians?

MIRANDA
I didn't have to – I *am* an Indian.

He lights the joint and inhales.

BOB STILLS
I wish I was an Indian.

MIRANDA
No, you don't.

BOB STILLS
I used to. I think every kid did really.

MIRANDA
Why's that?

BOB STILLS
Because they want to be free.

MIRANDA
That's like saying did you ever play Doctor, and then saying you always
wanted to be the patient.

BOB STILLS
What? Now that's fucked up …

MIRANDA
Really …

BOB STILLS

All I'm saying is that every kid playing Cowboys and Indians wanted to be the Indian because, one, it is funner, and two, you get to do what you want to do. An Indian gets to ride a wild horse, shoot bows and arrows; they get to tie people to stakes, and do the cool screams, scalp 'em, stab 'em, and dance, and sing, and smoke. That's a full afternoon of letting go if you ask me.

She doesn't laugh.

MIRANDA

I think I'm going to need a drag of that.

BOB STILLS

You're getting pissed off.

MIRANDA

No ... just /

BOB STILLS

/ Were you raised on a reservation?

MIRANDA

No, I was raised in a church that dressed itself like a school. There wasn't much freedom.

BOB STILLS

Your family?

MIRANDA

There wasn't much family. The church that dressed itself like a school also dressed itself like a jail. Three squares and three institutions for the price of one. Indian boarding school.

He takes off his headdress.

BOB STILLS

Believe it or not, I suddenly feel stupid ... you wanna go grab a drink?

MIRANDA

Like that?

BOB STILLS

Sure, why not … it would be good for me to see how the other half lives …

MIRANDA

You mean dies …

He reaches over and grabs a white Stetson.

BOB STILLS

If it makes you feel better, you can be the cowboy tonight …

He places it on her head. She grooves to it.

MIRANDA

I don't think you know what centuries of never wearing a white Stetson can do to a girl –

BOB STILLS

I'll take my chances.

MIRANDA leans in and kisses BOB STILLS dressed as an Indian.

Lights fade.

∼ Janey's Indian Room

SFX: The sound of the tide surging in and out.

JANEY lies heavily sedated on a stretcher covered by a white sheet, in an extremely white room. In a series of fades, TWO WHITE INTERNS hover over her body in different positions – moving, moving.

JANEY looks up and from a distance THE LONE WOMAN appears like a dream. She stands as a younger woman on the tide line of her island.

THE LONE WOMAN

(*Gabrielino*) Kohooke'aa'a.

JANEY responds across space.

JANEY

What did you say?

> The TWO WHITE INTERNS begin to unbutton her dress
> and touch her upper body.

THE LONE WOMAN

(*Gabrielino*) Kohooke'aa'a.

JANEY

I can't get what you are saying.

> THE LONE WOMAN smiles and responds in English.

THE LONE WOMAN

To hide.

> THE LONE WOMAN gets closer, smiling; she looks beautiful
> against the brilliant blue sky. The TWO WHITE INTERNS
> touch JANEY's abdomen.

JANEY

To hide …

> She moans in response to their touch.

THE LONE WOMAN

(*Gabrielino*) Tokuupanga.

JANEY

Please say it again …

> The TWO WHITE INTERNS draw her dress up and, taking
> a basin and washcloth, begin to wipe her abdomen and
> between her legs. The washcloth wrings out dark red.

THE LONE WOMAN

Look to the sky … Tokuupanga.

> The brilliant blue sky takes over the room.

JANEY

Tokuupanga. In the sky … The sky … please don't …

The TWO WHITE INTERNS put their hands inside her
as she moans and stares directly at THE LONE WOMAN
for help.

THE LONE WOMAN
(*Gabrielino*) Nataaxtax.

JANEY
My body.

THE LONE WOMAN
(*Gabrielino*) Kochooke'aa.

JANEY
To hide.

THE LONE WOMAN
(*Gabrielino*) Tokuupanga.

JANEY
In the sky.

THE LONE WOMAN
(*Gabrielino*) Ataatax.

JANEY
Her body.

THE LONE WOMAN
(*Gabrielino*) Kochooke'aa. Tokuupanga. Taatax.

> *The TWO WHITE INTERNS jab her deeply and JANEY*
> *jolts upwards, knocking over the water basin, splashing red*
> *over the blue. They dress her in a green hospital smock. She*
> *curls in a fetal position. DETECTIVE FULLEN enters and*
> *talks with the TWO WHITE INTERNS. He sits down beside*
> *JANEY, taking her hand.*

JANEY
Kochooke'aa. Tokuupanga. Netaaxtax. To hide … in the sky … of a
woman's body. To hide in the sky of a woman's body.

> *He touches her, strokes her hair as tears fall.*

DETECTIVE FULLEN

There was no baby, was there? … No baby because there was no way you could have conceived.

She doesn't respond.

You knew you were sterilized, didn't you? You knew but you let us believe you killed him, why?

She stares off into space not looking at him.

JANEY

I did conceive of him. I did. I wanted a baby … I wanted a baby … I always wanted a baby /

DETECTIVE FULLEN

/ It's not the same as having a baby /

JANEY

/ It is if it has to be.

He talks to her gently.

DETECTIVE FULLEN

It doesn't work that way.

JANEY

How do you know? /

DETECTIVE FULLEN

/ You didn't have a baby because it was physically impossible /

JANEY

/ How do you know how things work?

DETECTIVE FULLEN

/ You know that … you know that's the truth.

Pause. She begins to fall asleep.

JANEY

What does truth have to do with it … don't you understand anything?

DETECTIVE FULLEN

Juana …

JANEY

My name is Janey … My name is …

> *Exhausted, she falls into a deep sleep. Lights fade.*

～ Jessie's Indian Room

> *JESSIE stares out her office window. As clouds move across the glass, the reflection of a young Indian woman, SARAH, age eighteen, stands in the doorway. JESSIE, startled, turns around.*

JESSIE

You frightened me. I'm sorry, you're not supposed to be in here. We've closed for the day.

SARAH

There was no one at the receptionist's desk when I came in so I just walked through.

JESSIE

Uhmmm … Why don't you come back tomorrow and we'll /

> *SARAH looks down.*

SARAH

/ It's important.

> *JESSIE goes to turn on the desk lamp.*

Don't turn on the light. Please.

JESSIE

All right … What seems to be the problem?

SARAH

Actually … hmm … it's not a problem. I just wanted to come back and say … well … I'm ready …

JESSIE

I'm sorry … I don't know what you are talking about.

SARAH

My boyfriend and I are going to get married.

JESSIE

Can I get your name?

SARAH

My name is Sarah ... my boyfriend and I are going to get married and
I guess what I am trying to say is I'm ready to have a baby now ...

JESSIE

You're ready to get pregnant, Sarah? How old are you?

SARAH

I just turned eighteen. My boyfriend's older, though. He's twenty-two.

JESSIE

Have you been pregnant before, Sarah?

Embarrassed, SARAH talks on.

SARAH

Yes ... uhmmm ... twice. I ... wasn't thinking I guess ... I got myself
into a couple of situations and I had abortions because ... I just wasn't
able to look after them ... and ... the guys I was with ... uhm ...
well ... I'm just trying to say it's different now, and I'm going to get
married and I was wondering how long it would take before I could
get my womb transplant? And how long would it take for it to work?
My boyfriend ... husband ... wants children really bad too ...

There is a long pause. JESSIE begins to laugh.

JESSIE

This is a set-up, right? Daniel sent you to set me up?

SARAH responds with horrified silence.

SARAH

What?

JESSIE looks at her face and realizes it is real.

JESSIE

I'm sorry, I didn't mean to laugh ... It's just that ... uhmmm ... There's
no such thing as a womb transplant.

SARAH stares at her.

SARAH

What are you talking about? The last time I was in here the doctor said if I signed this paper they could help me ... because I kept getting pregnant ... and he said that ... they could stop me from having to go through that, and that I could just come back here and get my ... womb back when I was serious about my life.

JESSIE

I think there's been some kind of terrible misunderstanding. What doctor was this?

SARAH begins to get very upset.

SARAH

He said I could just come in and schedule it when I wanted to ... he said that it was a normal procedure and all I had to do was sign a paper and it would be fine ...

SARAH tries hard not to cry.

JESSIE

I'm sorry ... I don't know any doctor who could say that ... it's not possible.

SARAH

You calling me a liar?

JESSIE

No ... no ... I'm just saying what you're asking for is not done because it's physically impossible to transplant a womb.

SARAH gasps, falling back with the weight of it.

Why don't we turn the lights on ... and I can take a look at you ... obviously /

SARAH

/ And see what?

JESSIE reaches out to her and SARAH, seeing her hands, just stares at her.

JESSIE

I'm ... I ... /

SARAH

/ Your hands are brown just like mine.

JESSIE

I think maybe you should leave and you can come back tomorrow. We can go through the files and we can get to the bottom of this. There's got to be a record, an explanation.

JESSIE looks at her softly.

What was the doctor's name?

SARAH

What does it matter … you're all the same … I don't trust your white paper, and I don't trust a woman who wears white and has brown hands.

SARAH pushes JESSIE's hand away and backs away from her in disgust.

Lights fade.

∼ Miranda's Indian Room

MIRANDA and BOB STILLS walk into his modern apartment, furnished in white. It is messy with clothes, books, cowboy-and-Indian film posters. He grabs a bottle of vodka and pours them a healthy dose. He hands it to her, unsteady.

BOB STILLS

Don't worry about spilling anything … I do it all the time … You okay? … I'm shit-faced.

She takes a huge swig and looks at the movie posters with his name in big letters. He looks at her looking.

I'm a fuckin' cliché, really. Cheers to me … I mean, who would have thought I would be a slightly overweight fortysomething director, who hasn't directed a script in years … and then, when I do get my comeback, it's the same old crap that distorts history and the whole Indian–white man thing. I'm glad we met … so I could say this to someone … If I dropped dead tomorrow, my life's work would represent nothing but ... what? ... fuck, okay, okay ... completely honest ... a fuckin' red-and-white lie ... I said it.

She starts to speak but he is on a roll ...

I started out wanting to depict a time in history, a place, and ended up getting caught in the titles ... *The Sun Rises on the White Cowboy Hat*, *The White Man's Revenge*, *Massacre Where the Cow Crosses* ... I mean, shit ...

MIRANDA

I saw one of your films ... it was really beautiful ... really /

BOB STILLS

/ The art film. It totally fucked me. It was something. It was something. It was something I wanted to do my whole life and then I finally get the chance, and they just cut my balls off.

MIRANDA

Why?

BOB STILLS

Too political ... you can't do a film here that's gonna make people think. It's too dangerous.

MIRANDA

I'm sorry ...

He looks at her.

BOB STILLS

It's not your fault.

MIRANDA

I'm just sorry you didn't get what you wanted ... there's always time though ...

BOB STILLS almost cries.

You okay?

BOB STILLS

Yeah ... shit ... I look at you and I see how young you are ... just incredibly beautiful and ... hopeless.

MIRANDA

Thanks, I think … was that a compliment?

BOB STILLS

Yes … yes … it … is … You're right … it's not over until it's over.

MIRANDA

That's spoken like a true cowboy.

BOB STILLS

You wanna fight?

MIRANDA

You'd lose.

BOB STILLS

What makes you so sure?

MIRANDA

Because anyone who thinks winning, or losing, is a choice usually loses.

BOB STILLS

So, what about all your dead Indians, who were shot and killed in movies. They lost.

MIRANDA

Did they?

BOB STILLS

Of course. That's how it works. You die, you lose.

MIRANDA

You don't know much about Indians, do you?

BOB STILLS

Obviously, I don't know the right answer.

MIRANDA

That's a good start.

He sits down beside her.

BOB STILLS

Has anyone ever told you … you're beautiful?

MIRANDA

No.

BOB STILLS

Liar. Can I tell you something that sounds stupid?

MIRANDA

Sure.

BOB STILLS

I've always felt that there was a part of me that was Indian.

MIRANDA

You want to be part Indian even if you're a loser and die?

BOB STILLS

I didn't mean it that way …

MIRANDA

Maybe you're a closet Indian.

BOB STILLS

Very funny. What about you? What's in your closet?

MIRANDA

An Indian mother who was shot dead, and two sisters who have vanished.

BOB STILLS

I'm sorry.

MIRANDA

Winners should never say they're sorry.

BOB STILLS

Look at me, I'm not a winner … I'm … a has-been.

MIRANDA

Historically … so I am.

> She picks up a video camera.

MIRANDA
  This is cool …

BOB STILLS
  It is … if you want to, you can turn it on.

MIRANDA
  Really?

BOB STILLS
  Just be careful, it's heavy …

> *She turns on the switch and points the camera with the lens cap on.*

Here, I think maybe I should be the one who takes the picture … besides, you're prettier than me.

> *He takes the cap off and a live image of her projects on the wall.*

MIRANDA
  What do you want me to do?

BOB STILLS
  Just be yourself.

> *She smiles and begins to unbutton her blouse.*

Perfect.

> *BOB STILLS films, following her with the camera until he no longer can hold it. Lights fade.*

⌒ Janey's Indian Room

> *JANEY sits in the interview room dressed in plain, clean clothes. She looks up as DETECTIVE FULLEN enters.*

DETECTIVE FULLEN
  You look good … they're releasing you, Janey …

JANEY
  How did you know my name?

DETECTIVE FULLEN

You told me after your examination, and while you were in there I ran your name through Child Protective Services … You've had quite a few names …

JANEY

My real mother called me Janey … usually I just tell people they can call me whatever they want … everything's temporary anyways … I've been in twenty-six foster homes … it's not like it matters …

DETECTIVE FULLEN

I thought you were Mexican when you first came in … names are deceiving …

JANEY

The first family they placed me with was Chicano. They named me Juana Maria after the Lone Woman of San Nicolas Island. I guess they wanted to make me strong. It stuck to the paper …

DETECTIVE FULLEN

Did she stick to you?

JANEY

She's a part of my own story … She recognized what I needed … I needed to know what it felt like to hold my own child … even for a moment.

He looks at her.

DETECTIVE FULLEN

You didn't have a baby.

She looks at him.

JANEY

Didn't I? She placed him in my arms so I could feel the weight of my loss … Now I can mourn properly …

DETECTIVE FULLEN

Did she mourn her child properly?

JANEY

Why do you care?

DETECTIVE FULLEN

Because I want to know.

JANEY

Will knowing change anything …

> *Pause.*

DETECTIVE FULLEN

You can trust me …

> *Pause.*

JANEY

She mourned every day like it was yesterday.

> *JANEY looks over as THE LONE WOMAN comes into sight.*
> *DETECTIVE FULLEN looks over and finally sees her.*

DETECTIVE FULLEN

What /

∼ *Jessie's Indian Room*

DANIEL

/ What are you doing?

> *JESSIE is looking down in front of a locked filing cabinet.*

JESSIE

Trying to get this open …

DANIEL

It's locked … too many break-ins, so I put the files that aren't active in here …

> *She hesitates and looks at the filing cabinet one more time.*

Christ, what a long day, or should I say days. It's kinda like Las Vegas here. The day never ends, and every day looks the same … timeless.

> *He watches her as she sits down, uneasy.*

I had at least forty cases today and then one old Indian woman I thought was being abused because she had these huge blue bruises on her legs. I kept asking questions like "Have you had a fall lately, or did someone hurt you?" And every time she just nods her head, and finally I get her to walk around the office to see if she can show me where anything hurts, and I see this big blue stain on the pocket of her cardigan, and I ask her if I can take a look, and see what's in there. What do you think it is?

> *No response.*

It's a bingo marker with a broken tip busted off, and it has been leaking blue highlighter over everything. I pull it out of her pocket and she just smiles and says, "Bingo."

> *He laughs charmingly. She doesn't look at him.*

Not funny?

JESSIE
Something really disturbing happened when I was about to the leave the office.

> *He moves closer.*

DANIEL
Honey?

JESSIE
A woman, an Indian girl really, appeared out of nowhere ...

DANIEL
What happened, Jessie?

> *She looks directly at him.*

JESSIE
She asked for a womb transplant.

> *DANIEL pales and opens up a cabinet, taking out a bottle of scotch and a glass.*

DANIEL
A what?

JESSIE

A womb transplant ... she said that /

He nervously pours himself a drink.

DANIEL

/ Jessie ... she probably just walked off the streets, on drugs or
something ...

JESSIE

She wasn't on drugs ... she ...

He drinks his scotch.

Can I ask you a question?

DANIEL

You can ask me anything, Jessie ...

JESSIE

Is this really what you wanted? To head up an inner-city clinic in
L.A. ... not exactly the cash cow your father had planned for you
when you said you were going to medical school.

He casually answers, not missing a beat.

DANIEL

This is what I wanted ... it's an opportunity for me, for us, to make a
difference.

He walks around the space.

I grew up with everything from the moment I was conceived. *That* is
a privilege. I will never need for anything, never mind something as
fundamental as health care.

He looks at her.

Meeting you, getting to know you, loving you, has changed the way I
see things.

JESSIE

What do you mean?

DANIEL

I mean, look at you. The odds were against you being who you are
now. You and your sisters are separated, and you are placed in foster

care where you could have stayed till the end of time, but a decent white couple take you in, adopt you, raise you like their own. They provide you with what every child should have: a home, parents that love them, education, health care, security, and you become this young woman, this young Indian woman who becomes a doctor. One of the first Indian women doctors in America. *That's* something.

JESSIE

Daniel, you know I never grew up with my heritage.

DANIEL

You're telling me you forgot your whole childhood?

> *Irritated, she gets up.*

JESSIE

I'm telling you I had to forget the part of me that is Indian.

DANIEL

I don't think you forgot anything ... You're like the perfect story ... because you are the best of both worlds.

JESSIE

How can I be the best of both worlds when I can't even find my sisters ...

DANIEL

Isn't that why you're really here? You wanted to come here as bad as I did ... as a way of getting closer to your own people ... your own sisters. Working here has allowed you to help *these* people ...

JESSIE

/ Shut up ...

> *There is a long pause.*

DANIEL

What did you just say?

JESSIE

I said ...

> *Pause. He goes to her ...*

DANIEL

Jessie … come here … please … I know you're tired … Listen, I'm happy we can do this together … Whatever the reasons either of us has for being here, or whether we truly understand what our role is here … we can do something real. Something good.

JESSIE begins to leave.

JESSIE

I just … I just need to /

DANIEL

/ Jessie … don't go …

He seductively begins to unbutton her white coat and then her blouse.

Shhh … you just need me, Jessie … Just let me hold you …

JESSIE

Daniel, I … I …

DANIEL

I love you, Jessie … I do love you … let me love you …

She backs away but is seduced by him …

Lights fade.

The sound of them making love intertwines with the sound of BOB STILLS and MIRANDA making love, growing like waves under the following scene – live – as the couples make love in their own separate darkened rooms. A white light flickers like a bright sun in JANEY's room as it becomes an island, rich in colour like a vision becoming real.

THE LONE WOMAN

It was a hot day as far as the ocean was concerned. I was playing on the beach with my son, my silly boy, my rock. The wind whispered and I listened.

THE LONE WOMAN looks farther across the ocean and sees the faraway image of a boat.

DANIEL

(*offstage*) What would I do without you. You are mine.

> *The boat's bow beats against the deep-blue water and the wash of white spray as it crashes down in a constant rhythm.*

THE LONE WOMAN

I heard them approach over the waves. It was nothing new, as nothing is anymore. They had come to our island before, a long time ago, taking, and before that each time, taking more of us until there were fewer. They came.

> *BOB STILLS reaches over and pulls MIRANDA to him. The sound of their lovemaking joins the growing wave.*

BOB STILLS

(*offstage*) I need you. I need to …

> *MIRANDA grabs him in closer.*

> *JESSIE holds her hand against DANIEL's chest.*

DANIEL

(*offstage*) I love you. Please.

> *Her hand lets go and DANIEL advances.*

THE LONE WOMAN

They came. I hid my child under the roots of a tree like I'd done before. I hid him with deep plans to come back when things were safe for him to live. I hid my son, then stood like I was ready to be took to the mainland with the others.

MIRANDA

(*offstage*) Can you see me? Can you really see what's inside of me?

JESSIE

(*offstage*) Just tell me it will be all right … please. Just tell me …

> *THE LONE WOMAN sits in a boat and then suddenly stands up into a dark and stormy sky.*

> *SFX: The sound of a child's cry.*

THE LONE WOMAN

They rowed me far from shore … his cries reached inside of me … I stood up and heard him …

BOB STILLS

(*offstage*) Please …

> *THE LONE WOMAN stands on the boat and begins to fall back into the ocean in slow motion. As she does, JESSIE and DANIEL, BOB STILLS and MIRANDA let their bodies fall back and away from each other. THE LONE WOMAN falls deep into the ocean.*

THE LONE WOMAN

I fell back, swimming back, all the while feeling the hot sun and the coarse sand … willing the feeling of his cool skin as he climbs onto me … both of us crying like the first time we met …

> *She emerges, standing wet and alone on the beach, almost not breathing.*

I went back. I went back … I went back to our island … no matter how long I looked … he was gone … eaten by wild dogs … or drowned …

> *She looks at DETECTIVE FULLEN. She bends down and writes her last-known words in the sand.*

> *SLIDE (text)*
> Kohooke'aa'a. Tokuupar. Taatax.

Even though they hadn't been able to take him … they were able to take my child from me. So when the Takers came again, I stood still. The only one left on this island. The last of my people to be taken.

> *She stands up and looks into THE BLACKCOATS as they approach her. The scene freezes into a nicely painted and lighted diorama.*

> *JANEY looks over at DETECTIVE FULLEN, who moves towards THE LONE WOMAN, looking at her.*

DETECTIVE FULLEN

What happened to her?

JANEY

Alone. She was the last one taken to the mainland. She was taken, dressed for an exhibit, and documented. She died six weeks later ...

He bends down and traces the words in the sand, trying to make sense of them.

DETECTIVE FULLEN

Kohooke'aa'a. Tokuupar. Taatax. To hide ... in the sky ... of a woman's body. To hide in the sky of a woman's body ... Why do you think these were the only words she spoke, the last words they documented? What was she trying to tell them?

JANEY

They think they took everything ... but you cannot take the sky.

JANEY looks up at the sky.

SFX: The sound of thunder.

You know the story you told about your grandfather's Indian Room ... that you were scared of the darkness under the chair ... the darkness in the room ...

DETECTIVE FULLEN

Yes ...

JANEY

The tears of Indians are gathering ...

She looks at him.

And there will be a flood no room can contain.

SFX: Sound of rain falling under.

JANEY walks forward and touches the glass as rain begins to fall; at the same time MIRANDA slowly removes herself from BOB STILLS and walks towards the glass, touching it, as JESSIE gets up from DANIEL and walks towards the glass, touching it.

In my Indian Room, I constructed my own island. Like the Lone Woman before me, I watched outside of myself, an ocean between me, and them. They had come like a child trying to sneak up on a secret.

Noisy enough, but I did not know there were those who could steal dreams from the sky. Now, in my Indian Room, I do not hide myself but open myself up to the blue – a possibility that something that loved in me can live again somewhere.

> *JANEY begins to draw.*

> *SLIDE (image)*
>> An island, and then a sun, a child, and a mother and a long cord connecting.

MIRANDA

In my Indian Room, there was nothing in me to go to, or from. The earth was red with blood spilled and the souls of untouched feet walked upon it, as if nothing had ever happened. As if they had been baptized by the floods, forgiven without admission, released without being held. Now in *my* Indian Room, I walk the bloody walk, and wipe my feet at their door, not to track blood on to their shiny new floors.

> *MIRANDA begins to draw.*

> *SLIDE (image)*
>> Crude images of cowboys and Indians, bows and arrows, horses and guns and, finally, dead bodies on the ground.

JESSIE

In my Indian Room, my mother's voice cried in me day after day to hold on. The marrow of her scream has gotten into my bones, so long ago. Despite me, it has grown its own loud skeleton in me. It has grown its own brown flesh, my hands becoming hers. Now, in my Indian Room, I can hear their voices growing inside me, growing arms and legs, growing hands like mine, that want to touch, to grab on to, hold on to the impossible.

> *JESSIE takes her rock and opens the locked filing cabinet. She shakily goes through the files. She begins to write.*

> *SLIDE (image)*
>> Names of women patients, their ages, and sterilization dates appear as statistics that begin to fill the wall.

Blackout.

⁓ Miranda's Indian Room

*MIRANDA looks out through the glass wall of MIRANDA's
INDIAN ROOM and over at BOB STILLS, who is passed
out on his couch.*

MIRANDA

I dreamed once I had a mother, and she had me, and I had two sisters
and she had them, and we were on a bus, with a skinny grey dog on
the side, and my older sister looked smart looking out the window,
but I barfed on the floor, and it felt good, and my other sister buried
her baby face in my mother's deep breast, and drank like that river
was hers. I dreamed once I had a mother and she had me, and I had
two sisters, and she had them, and we were on a bus with a skinny
grey dog on the side, and we were travelling a long way to make a liar's
story, and it was hot and my mother opened the bus window and a
beautiful stream of wind came on us, and it blew my mother's black
hair all over our round faces, which lay on my mother's body, like we
owned her. She said just then, "Look, girls, look at those rocks." These
three big boulders standing just so in the desert, staring just enough
for us to recognize them. She said, "Miranda, don't you recognize
them from home? Look how they stand," and I said, "Yes, I think I do."
She said, "Miranda, the rock family is following us to L.A. to start a
new life too. Maybe they can be our neighbours." Such are the things
memories are made of.

She quietly begins to pick up her clothes from the floor.

BOB STILLS

Where you going? Come on … don't leave … come back …

MIRANDA

It's all right, I was just getting my stuff together.

BOB STILLS

I'm sorry.

MIRANDA

For what?

BOB STILLS

Getting too drunk. Taking too many drugs. Talking too much ... I forget what I'm supposed to be sorry for.

MIRANDA

It's all right ...

BOB STILLS

No, it isn't ... Come on ...

MIRANDA

No ... I just need to get going ... and think through some stuff ...

BOB STILLS

Listen ... I said I was sorry ...

MIRANDA

You don't have to be sorry. It's nothing. It's fine / I just need ...

BOB STILLS

/ "It's nothing ... it's fine ..." What's that supposed to mean?

MIRANDA

Bob ... You're not hearing me ... Everything's cool ... I just /

BOB STILLS

/ What, you think I think this was nothing?

MIRANDA

You're kidding me, right?

BOB STILLS

Do I look like I'm kidding you?

MIRANDA

No, you look like you're going to have a heart attack.

BOB STILLS

That's funny ... considering I have a heart condition.

His face goes white.

MIRANDA

Is it? It's a saying /

BOB STILLS
/ That's really fuckin' funny.

MIRANDA
Okay, you know what? I think, it was a really interesting evening ...

BOB STILLS
What?

MIRANDA
I said /

BOB STILLS
/ Interesting ... "Interesting" means you suck, in my business.

MIRANDA
What?

BOB STILLS
"Interesting" equals "suck."

MIRANDA
Uhmmm. Okay. All right. I don't need this right now. Why don't
you get over your hangover, or whatever ... and we can talk later on,
okay ... thanks for the evening ...

> BOB STILLS looks coldly at MIRANDA.

BOB STILLS
So you think you can just use me?

MIRANDA
Pardon me?

BOB STILLS
I said do you think that you can just walk in here and do anything you
like and just leave. I guess you think because you're Indian you can do
anything you want ...

MIRANDA
What the fuck are you talking about?

BOB STILLS

Fuck … I guess I'm supposed to feel sorry for you. What was it … you said your mother was what … shot?

MIRANDA

She came here in the fifties when they loaded a bunch of Indians on a bus and drove them to L.A. to make a living. To become civilized like you.

BOB STILLS

Clever … Did she?

MIRANDA

She tried /

BOB STILLS

/ Let me guess … It's an Indian classic. She couldn't get a job. She had what? … three kids … no money … She got depressed, starting drinking, leaving her kids alone …

MIRANDA

She never left us alone … She was a good mother … Asshole.

BOB STILLS

At least, you've got the right pronunciation …

MIRANDA

How's "fuck you" … for intention.

BOB STILLS

Fuck you too …

She watches as BOB STILLS pushes Rewind on the video recorder.

MIRANDA

What are you doing?

BOB STILLS

I think I can make a few dollars out of our cultural exchange …

MIRANDA

What are you talking about?

BOB STILLS

The camera was rolling … don't be so naive.

MIRANDA

You can't do that.

BOB STILLS

Sure I can.

MIRANDA

You barely got it up.

BOB STILLS

What did I tell you about make-believe? I think I can doctor it up bit.
You know, put in a few drumbeats and maybe add a few scenes with
you or someone like you wearing a buckskin dress … I think I will
call it … *Princess Redfeather*. Everybody likes to see an Indian getting
fucked.

MIRANDA

Is that right?

> *SFX: The tape clunks to a stop.*

> *They barely breathe as the tape moves forward and into the
> intimate sounds of lovemaking under. Shadows of them
> reflect across the room. He turns away, watching the scene.*

BOB STILLS

I think it's beautiful … raw, savage, but to the point.

> *She moves towards him.*

MIRANDA

Give me the tape.

BOB STILLS

I don't think so.

MIRANDA

Give me the tape, or I will …

BOB STILLS

What? What, Miranda … What will you do?

> *Pause.*

MIRANDA

I will kill you.

∼ Janey's Indian Room

> *DETECTIVE FULLEN looks at JANEY. He moves towards her ...*

DETECTIVE FULLEN

What about you, Janey? Did you go back to find out what happened to your baby?

> *She looks at him and then touches her belly.*

Janey?

JANEY

I wasn't feeling well ... I felt like I was burning up, so I went back to the clinic and I said /

> *She is barely able to continue.*

DETECTIVE FULLEN

/ You said /

JANEY

/ I said ... something is wrong ... Something is so hollow ... Something is wrong ... wrong ... wrong ... I went back ... I went back ...

> *JANEY walks to JESSIE'S INDIAN ROOM. DETECTIVE FULLEN follows.*

I went back to her ...

∼ Jessie's Indian Room

> *JANEY enters. There is blood flowing down her legs and staining her dress.*

JESSIE

Oh, my God, you're bleeding, what happened?

> *JESSIE grabs a towel.*

JANEY

He took something from inside me ... You have to fix it ... please ...

JESSIE

You're bleeding ... here ... let me ...

JANEY backs away.

JANEY

Where are my babies going to live? Where are my babies going to
live ... Tell me where my babies are going to live ...

She looks down.

JESSIE

I ... I don't know what ...

JESSIE tries not to look at her directly.

JANEY

Look me in the eye ... and tell me you don't know what I am talking
about.

*JESSIE finally looks directly at JANEY. They take each other
in.*

JESSIE

I'm sorry ... so sorry ...

*JANEY and JESSIE hold their gaze, remembering each as
sisters through the following scene.*

JANEY

I dreamed once I had a mother, and she had me, and I had two sisters
and she had them, and we were on a bus, with a skinny grey dog on
the side, and my older sister was looking smart out the window, and
my other sister barfed on the floor, and it smelled, so I buried my baby
face in my mother's deep breast, and drank like that river was mine. I
dreamed once I had a mother, and she had me, and I had two sisters,
and she had them, and we were on a bus with a skinny grey dog on
the side, and we were travelling a long way to make a new beginning,
and it was hot and my mother opened the bus window, and a beautiful
stream of wind came over us, and it blew my mother's black hair all

over our round faces, which lay on my mother's body, like we owned her. She said just then, "Look, girls, look at those rocks." These three big boulders standing just so in the desert, staring just enough for us to recognize them. She said, "Janey, baby, look. Don't you recognize them from home? Look how they stand," and I thought, "Yes, I think I do." She said /

JESSIE

/ She said ... "Janey, baby, the rock family is following us to L.A. to start a new life too ..." Such are the things memories are made of.

JANEY

And I said ... "Look, Jessie, look at me ... don't you recognize me ... don't you recognize me from home ... Look how I stand ..."

JESSIE

And ... I said ... "Yes ... I think I do."

JANEY

Maybe we could have been sisters ... Such are the things memories are made of.

> *JESSIE watches as JANEY begins to leave her room ... grabbing her rock ... she begins to unravel.*

JESSIE

Maybe we could have been sisters ... Such are the things memories are made of ... Maybe we could have been ... maybe we could have been sisters ... maybe ...

> *DANIEL enters.*

DANIEL

Jessie? Jessie ... What's wrong? Jessie? Jessie, answer ... me ... answer me now!

> *She looks at her glass wall covered with the names of women patients. Grabbing her rock, she throws it at the glass, breaking an opening.*
>
> *SFX: The sound of glass breaking.*
>
> *SFX: The sound of drums beating.*

SFX: *The sound of water pouring down.*

DANIEL begins to approach her calmly.

Let's just sit … take a minute, Jessie, and calm down …

She backs away from him.

JESSIE

Calm down … calm down … you calm down … you're so good at talking, Daniel …

DANIEL

Jesus Christ, Jessie, it's me, what you are doing?

JESSIE

When were you going to tell me, Daniel? When were you going to tell me you are sterilizing brown women. Indian women.

Taken aback, he tries to gather himself.

DANIEL

Jessie, you have to understand … This is government / policy

JESSIE

/ Paper /

DANIEL

/ I am on contract like a thousand other doctors across the country … all right, here … Take your background … Now … what if someone would have given your mother the option of not having to care and fend for three children? She might of lived.

Pause.

Instead, she died in poverty, and violence, and left her children to the same fate. What we are offering here is birth control so that the population will not be infected by people who cannot control their urges …

JESSIE

Have I infected you, Daniel?

DANIEL

What are you talking about?

JESSIE

You made my family an example of infection … Have I infected you by being alive, Daniel?

DANIEL

Jessie, I never … said that … you're taking this way too personally, you have to look at the big picture.

She looks right in him.

JESSIE

I saw the big picture today … Daniel …

He looks at her.

I found my sister … I met my sister and she had blood coming from her … you have my sister's blood on your hands … You want to know the last thing I can remember my mother saying was … "Hold Janey now … Hold her … hold her …

DANIEL

We can get through this, Jess … We can pretend it didn't happen. I can do that, Jess …

JESSIE

"Remember my hands, Jessie … remember to keep me inside /

He moves towards her as she climbs up on a chair close to the broken window.

DANIEL

/ Jessie … listen to yourself … you're not making any sense … For Christ's sake, Jessie … I'm done talking to you … Get down now! I said now!

She looks out the window and leans her body out.

Jessie, please … Jessie, look at me …

She looks at him but doesn't see him.

JESSIE

I don't see you now /

DANIEL

/ You can't do this …

JESSIE

I want to go back. / I want to go back.

DANIEL

/ I love you, Jessie … for fuck's sake get down … please /

JESSIE

/ Falling back /

DANIEL

/ I'm sorry …

JESSIE

Falling back to hold on /

DANIEL

/ Do you want me to beg …? / I'll beg, okay, Jessie …

JESSIE

Hold on /

DANIEL

/ I'll do what you want …

JESSIE

Let go of the lies.

DANIEL

Jessie, give me a chance /

JESSIE

/ A chance to feel the river again at my feet.

> *He reaches to her softly. She steps back on the chair and opens her arms. The chair tilts and suspends … He reaches out suspended.*

DANIEL

No …

> *JESSIE's body falls back and into a dark sky as DANIEL falls to the floor.*

THE LONE WOMAN

(*voiceover*) River made of dreams. Blood. Rain made of tears. Body. Thunder made of stone. Let the river sink into its soil.

The scene freezes into a nicely painted and lighted diorama.

⌒ Miranda's Indian Room

SFX: The sound of thunder and pouring rain increases.

SFX: The sound of drums intensifies.

MIRANDA is pointing a gun at BOB STILLS.

BOB STILLS

Okay … I get the irony, okay … Clever. Put the fuckin' gun down.

The sounds from the taped intimacy intensify as their breathing becomes louder and the sound of horses riding hard transform under.

MIRANDA

Take the tape out, Bob … Bob!

He holds his chest.

BOB STILLS

I don't feel so well.

MIRANDA

Take the tape out, now!

BOB STILLS goes over and takes the tape out.

Put it on the coffee table.

He bends down and places the tape on the coffee table. As he rises, he lunges for her and they struggle. Two gunshots go off. One hits the glass, breaking a hole that creates a wind tunnel. Air blows through and we hear the sound of rushing water. The other hits the TV, shattering the tube as the sound and shape of shadows distort from it. They look at each other. They back away. MIRANDA's dress is soaked with blood.

BOB STILLS

Oh fuck … oh no … no …

He grabs her as she slowly falls to her knees.

THE LONE WOMAN

(*voiceover*) River made of dreams. Blood. Rain made of tears. Body. Thunder made of stone. Let the river sink into its soil.

BOB STILLS begins to back away from the TV as the flickering shadows begin to take the shape of a million Indians on horseback riding towards him. He falters back, holding on to his chest. The scene freezes into a nicely painted and lighted diorama.

JANEY and DETECTIVE FULLEN stand in the space as both dioramas begin to fade into darkness. JANEY looks at DETECTIVE FULLEN and down at his tape recorder and pad of paper.

JANEY

Did you get everything you came for?

DETECTIVE FULLEN

I'm not the collector.

JANEY

Is that what you are going to say when they come?

DETECTIVE FULLEN bends down to the water and lays down his tape recorder and pen and paper inside the swirling water.

SFX: The sound of singing submerges under.

JANEY begins to move from him and towards the flow of the river.

DETECTIVE FULLEN

I'm going to say my grandfather collected Indian things because he loved them … not the things so much but the spirit left in them. I am going to say I am not my grandfather … I am going to say when someone we love is taken from us we begin to arrange their things like an altar in our home. We place their favourite rock, their lock of hair, their picture close to us, and this collection grows so much they become alive again in our presence ... so alive we can say ... I remember you ... I recognize you as a part of myself /

JANEY

/ Because I have kept you inside from the beginning ...

The water begins to rise.

She took us here when there was nowhere else to go. She took us here under everything and inside the waterways we called the tombs. She took us underground ...

From the darkness, MIRANDA appears and stands beside her sister.

MIRANDA

And inside the dreams of Indians ... It was dark ...

From the darkness, JESSIE appears and stands beside her sisters.

JESSIE

But inside the bowels of the river, we stood as streams of water flowed around our small bare feet, it felt cool and the dreams of our feet talked to the water ... and the water made a current that moved around three small boulders that were our bodies ...

MIRANDA

This watery whisper grew around us, and became a river ...

JESSIE

We didn't know what was to come.

JANEY

We didn't know the river rising beneath us was the tears of Indians ...

MIRANDA

We didn't know ...

JESSIE, MIRANDA, and JANEY

We didn't know ...

JANEY

   … until we had joined the flood.

> *The river of tears takes over everything, and in a series of*
> *fades, the silhouettes of the three sisters fade under the water,*
> *then reappear as three boulders.*

> *Darkness.*

Marie Clements is an award-winning performer, writer, director, producer, and co-director of red diva projects and frog girl films. As a writer, Marie's work has garnered numerous productions, publications, and awards, including the 2004 Canada-Japan Literary Award for *Burning Vision* and two shortlisted nominations for the Governor General's Award for Drama, in 2004 for *Burning Vision* and in 2008 for *Copper Thunderbird*. Marie has worked extensively in and across a variety of mediums, including theatre, performance, film, new media, radio, and television.